THE MARKETING HANDBOOK

A guide for voluntary and
non-profit making organisations

by Rosalind Druce and Stephen Carter

NEC

National Extension College
in association with
Channel Four Television Company Limited
and
Yorkshire Television Limited

CONTENTS

	Page
Introduction	1
Chapter 1 - *Your marketing strategy*	5
Chapter 2 - *Simple marketing research*	13
Chapter 3 - *Identifying target audiences*	25
Chapter 4 - *Designing your total offer*	33
Chapter 5 - *Promotions*	43
Chapter 6 - *Planning your marketing*	59
Bibliography	65
Useful contacts	68

INTRODUCTION

In the last few years 'marketing' has entered the language, and increasingly the practice, of the non-profit and social organisations. Marketing directors have been appointed by large charities, marketing departments are now standard parts of local authorities, and arts organisations have had to become increasingly aware of the pressures of the marketplace.

So what is marketing?

Marketing is fundamentally about people – finding out about people's needs and wants and developing effective ways of meeting these. It involves identifying the specific groups of people that an organisation is best placed to assist or attract, and providing services or products that meet their particular needs. Marketing is about *communicating* with different groups of people. It is also about ensuring that changes in people's requirements and interests, as well as the many social, economic and other changes that take place, are not threats to the existence of an organisation, but opportunities for developing new and more appropriate products and services.

> **Nelson and Colne College was faced with the problem of developing a service to meet a new need – the need for unemployed people to be trained or retrained in up-to-date skills. The college wanted the service to be accessible to local people and to encourage adults in the area to try out new skills. In 1984 it opened the Drop-in Skills Centre (DISC) which offered:**
>
> - **free advice to small businesses**
> - **help with English**
> - **an attractive reception area where adults could order courses by the hour**
> - **training packages to allow trainees to learn at their own pace**
> - **the option of trying as many courses as clients liked.**
>
> **All were designed to meet the needs of local adults and to ensure that the centre was as attractive, easy to use and accessible as possible.**

DISC is an example of marketing at its best; putting the 'customer' first in all aspects of the centre's work and evolving to meet new customer needs.

All non-profit-making and social groups are set up to assist, appeal to or influence particular groups of people; and to meet the needs or interests of these target groups. People's needs may be quite fundamental, such as good housing or healthcare, or they may be for education or entertainment. Whatever the nature of your organisation, you exist not to make profits, but to meet a particular set of social aims and objectives.

For profit-making businesses, marketing is a part of the management function and is responsible for identifying and satisfying customer requirements profitably. It can often appear to be about finding ways to sell people services they don't really want or need; and for this reason many people working in social organisations are wary of marketing. However, good marketing is fully compatible with the aims of social organisations and, indeed, is a key to ensuring that these aims are met.

What marketing is not about is finding ways to sell people services they don't really want or need. Despite this, many people working in voluntary or social organisations are unaware of what marketing can do for them.

Why is marketing so important?

The General, Municipal, Boilermakers and Allied Trades Union (GMB for short) was faced with the problem of falling membership. Through market research the GMB discovered that it had a lot to offer but that it was not communicating it in a language that appealed to new and potential members, in particular women and part-time workers. As a result the GMB decided to change its image and identity. A new name, logo, and slogan 'GMB – working together', presented the union as modern, moving with the times, and aware of its members' different interests. Further research was conducted to assess the impact of the new identity and to ensure that its objectives were achieved.

By taking a marketing approach the uncertainty and risk that may currently be part of your work is greatly removed. Are you reaching the people you want to reach? Is your membership growing or contracting? Do you know why? Is your product or service right for clients' or audiences' needs? Are you maximising gifts from donors? Why do they give to you? Do your press releases attract media interest? Are you using your promotional materials effectively? All these can be answered by taking a marketing approach.

By gaining a better understanding of your clients' or donors' needs and requirements you can more efficiently use your energies and resources to reach them. You can avoid the waste of redundant services, irrelevant information, unnecessary advertising, or poorly attended events. Marketing research can challenge assumptions about who you attract and what it is about you that attracts them. You can also use it to find out the potential of particular types of funders and donors.

Most important, good marketing gives you a greater chance of surviving. By identifying the wider changes that will affect your organisation, your clients and your donors – including political, economic and social developments – you can establish plans of action that will enable your organisation to respond to new challenges and difficulties.

Setting targets and developing a marketing strategy gives direction to an organisation, motivates staff, assists in providing a more effective service, improves communication with clients, donors and the public, gives an opportunity to monitor successes and failures, and provides useful feedback to donors and funders.

The role of The Marketing Handbook

The Marketing Handbook is designed for workers in voluntary and non-profit organisations who want to gain an understanding of what marketing is all about. These may be charities, local authorities, arts organisations, community centres, campaigning groups, trade unions, support networks, advisory bodies, or societies.

Each chapter takes you step-by-step through the marketing process, explaining what marketing is and how it relates to non-profit organisations. Selected case-studies drawn from the YTV/Channel 4 series *The Marketing Mix – Social Variety,* show the advantages of adopting a marketing approach to your work. The handbook is intended to be practical and accessible; avoiding jargon unless it is absolutely necessary, and assuming no prior knowledge or experience of a marketing approach.

Not all your organisation's marketing questions can be answered in such a short book. We hope, however, that *The Marketing Handbook* will convince you of the benefits of a marketing approach, act as a guide to good practice, and develop a continuing interest in marketing.

Chapter by chapter, through practical exercises, checklists and examples, the book takes you through the process of planning and implementing a marketing strategy. The first chapter begins by looking at the foundations of a marketing strategy – at defining what an organisation does, whom it offers services to, and who is competing with it for the time, money and attention of clients or donors. Chapter 1 also examines the external and internal factors that must be taken into account when planning and meeting objectives.

Subsequent chapters continue the marketing planning process. There is practical information on how to conduct simple marketing research, on designing the various ingredients of your product or service 'mix', on planning an effective promotional strategy, and on the methods you follow to design, implement and monitor a marketing strategy for your organisation. In the final section we indicate a range of reference books and resources that you may find of additional use.

We hope that it will excite an interest in marketing, and convince people working in voluntary, arts and non-profit organisations of the benefits of a marketing approach.

CHAPTER 1

Contents   *Page*

Where are you now?   7
The world outside   8
Inside your organisation   9
The SWOT analysis   9
Summary   11

Introduction

The phrase 'marketing strategy' may sound daunting. However, like many activities, there are a few standard rules and some tricks of the trade which can help you. For each activity there is a starting point and a destination. Your strategy is simply the route you follow to get from A to B.

This chapter focuses on the starting points for a sound marketing strategy. It will help you:

- assess where you are now
- identify some of the factors, both external and internal, that will shape your marketing strategy
- look at your goals
- identify a clear route to get you to your goals.

WHERE ARE YOU NOW?

To clarify where you are now, ask yourself:

[?] What does my organisation do?
[?] Who are my clients?
[?] Who else is offering the same service?

Spend some time thinking through your answers before reading on.

What does your organisation do?

What you do can't be divorced from who you do it *for*. A hospital provides health care for people needing treatment for illness and injury. A museum provides exhibits, events, and information to people wanting education and entertainment.

How did you get to this point?

Being clear about what you do and the reasons and decisions that have brought you to this point, will help you review your current position. Identifying the role of the organisation is the first step to identifying potential clients, funders, and competitors. And it is your knowledge of these that will shape the strategy you decide to follow.

Who are your clients?

Many organisations feel they know who their clients are; that is the people or organisations who buy or take up their service, activities or facilities. They may feel confident also about what services or information clients need. But, sometimes feelings can become out-of-date or be based on inaccurate assumptions. Testing out such impressions can be done by checking internal information and questioning staff or members of the public themselves. Doing simple marketing research is covered in Chapter 2.

Identifying clearly your clients or **target audience** is the first step to understanding what will persuade them to use your services and what will interest them in what you have to offer. We will look at how to find out more about your clients in Chapter 3. However, it's worth asking yourself now:.

[?] Who are my main clients?
[?] How detailed is my knowledge of them?
[?] Why do they use my service?

(Is this because there is no other organisation vying for their attention or because they prefer the service you offer to the alternatives?)

Who else is offering the same service?

The days of the state monopoly are numbered; every institution from a water authority to a housing organisation has to face the fact of competition.

Any organisation which competes for the time, money, attention and effort of your supporters, clients and public–funding bodies is in competition with you. A charity such as the World Wildlife Fund cannot avoid competing with many other charities for money, for media coverage, and for people's interest.

Temba Theatre Company is besieged on all sides as it tries to provide a new, positive image for UK blacks:
- **it is forced to compete with other theatres and art forms for Arts Council funding.**
- **it competes for an audience with other forms of entertainment, such as other theatres, TV, nightclubs, eating out, concerts, etc.**
- **it is competing with all the traditional images of black Africa.**

Identifying your competitors is important for three main reasons:

1. So that you are complementing rather than duplicating the efforts of other organisations.

2. So that you can differentiate yourself from other organisations and create a very clear identity for yourself - in the commercial world this is known as **branding** and it works!

3. For straightforward business reasons, to get the lion's share of a potential market, whether this be maximising your share of public donations to a particular charitable cause or the local market for evening entertainment.

Try listing all the organisations that you compete with:

[?] Who else provides a similar service?
[?] Who else is competing for the attention and money of your clients or funders?

This list could prove to be very long!

Let's look now at other important factors that will shape your marketing strategy.

THE WORLD OUTSIDE

All of us know the impact of the world outside on our work. Political events may affect our activities or where our funds come from. Movements or changes in population may drastically increase or decrease the clients we serve. Such changes are called **uncontrollable variables**. While we cannot control them we must be aware of their happening and aim to make opportunities of the changes that occur.

Uncontrollable variables include:

- political events
- economic trends
- social and cultural changes
- technological progress
- legislative changes
- changes in lifestyles and attitudes
- changes in existing competition
- changes in funders' policies.

These factors – and you may be able to add others of your own – can have a positive or constraining effect on the nature of the services you are able to provide. For example, printers are affected strongly by rapidly changing printing technology. In turn this affects print trade unions and the services they provide to their members. Aid organisations supplying money and resources to a region suffering famine can easily be affected by political changes in the recipient country.

How could each of the uncontrollable variables listed above affect your organisation in the next few years. Is your organisation prepared for them?

INSIDE YOUR ORGANISATION

As well as looking outside your organisation you must also assess your internal variables (resources). These include:

- staff ability and numbers
- financial resources
- enthusiasm and commitment for the work
- networks
- your management skills
- image
- reputation
- the knowledge and information you have accumulated
- other capabilities and limitations.

THE SWOT ANALYSIS

A very useful and simple tool for assessing your current position in relation to your internal resources and the outside world is known as the SWOT analysis, in which you list your:

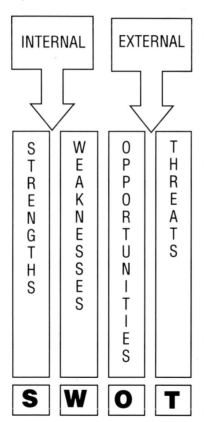

Make a list of the strengths and weaknesses of your organisation and the opportunities and threats presented by external events.

Out of the points you have noted, which are your key strengths and weaknesses in relation to your competition? Key strengths should be used to sell your organisation. Key weaknesses that might prevent clients from using you or send them elsewhere need to be identified and ways found to overcome them.

Strengths
These are the internal strengths of my organisation - how can we make them work harder for us?

Weaknesses
These are the internal weaknesses of my organisation. What must we do to improve in these areas and turn our weaknesses to strengths?

Opportunities
These are the external opportunities I can see arising for my organisation. How can we take most advantage of them?

Threats
These are the external threats facing my organisation. How can we prepare for them and turn them to our advantage?

Some weaknesses may also be strengths in different circumstances. For example, a large organisation may have security of large resources but may be very impersonal and slow to change. A small organisation, however, while lacking the financial resources may be quicker off the mark and able to adapt to change.

Checking out your objectives

The purpose of a marketing strategy is to get you from A to B. We have looked at how to identify where you are now, and the factors that affect your organisation. Now let's look at your objectives, or what you want to achieve.

All organisations have aims. A theatre may aim to provide live entertainment in order to promote certain issues to the public. A hospital will aim to provide professional medical assistance and facilities to particular groups of people, perhaps living within a specific area.

However, these broad aims are insufficient when it comes to planning and pursuing a marketing strategy. It is vital to set clear **objectives**, with measurable **targets** attached.

A charity may have as its broad aim the provision of advice and support to elderly disabled people. Its objectives, or what it seeks to achieve over the next few years, may include increasing the numbers of clients receiving a particular service, establishing support groups in particular areas, changing Government policy on an issue affecting clients, raising funds and recruiting volunteers.

The next step is to:

- attach clear marketing targets to each of these objectives
- set a time-scale for achieving these targets.

For example, the charity, in the next year, will plan to attract 100 new clients to the service, to establish ten support groups in specified areas, and to convince 30 influential politicians of its case for a policy change.

By setting clear targets you can monitor your progress and assess the success of your strategies. As well as ensuring that you do meet your objectives, this contributes to high morale among staff and demonstrates to your clients and funders that you are dynamic and moving with the times.

To be effective, marketing targets must be:

- measurable
- achievable
- desirable
- realistic

As an example let's examine the South Bank Centre's organisational objectives and marketing targets.

The South Bank Centre is the largest arts centre in the world. Its market research showed that the makeup of its audience was mainly the upper social classes, the so-called A, B and C1 classes, and that other social classes were not visiting it due to prejudice, ignorance and inertia. The Greater London Council required it to provide a programme of interest to all classes.

It therefore decided on the following objectives:

1. To provide a programme of events which would appeal to all social classes

2. To increase the number of people visiting the centre.

The first step taken to achieve this goal was to run an advertising and promotion campaign to overcome the lack of knowledge about its location and facilities.

Research showed that as a result of the campaign the proportion of the audience from the lower social classes increased. Numbers of under 25s also rose significantly.

Write down your organisational objectives

- List your marketing targets for, say, the next year, or a period that is relevant to you

- Ensure that your targets meet the four criteria: measurable, achievable, desirable, and realistic

If they don't, change your targets!

You are now ready to begin the process of drawing up a marketing strategy to reach your targets.

Let's summarise what we have covered so far before we move on.

SUMMARY

This chapter has aimed to help you lay the foundations for a sound marketing strategy. Like any activity, good preparation at the beginning paves the way for success at the end. Before continuing, check that you have now:

- *defined what your organisation does, who you offer services to, and who is competing with you for their time, money or attention*

- *examined the external and internal factors that affect your organisation and its work*

- *identified the objectives of your organisation, and clearly identified the targets that you plan to achieve.*

Later on we shall continue with the marketing planning process.

The following two chapters will provide more detailed answers to the questions about your markets, customers and competitors; Chapter 2 on simple techniques of market research and Chapter 3 on segmenting your target audience.

CHAPTER 2

Contents   *Page*

What is marketing research?   15
Why do marketing research?   15
Setting objectives   16
Planning   16
Action   22
Reviewing your results   22
Summary   24

Introduction

Anyone involved in making decisions will know the value of accurate and up-to-date information. The better the information, the more likely you are to achieve your aims. The risk of making costly mistakes can be avoided and more effective strategies formulated by planning and undertaking some simple marketing research.

In this chapter we look at when, why and how to carry out simple marketing research exercises. It will help you:

- use and collect information from your own records or other published sources
- use some of the key methods of conducting primary research, such as using questionnaires or simple observation.

But first, let's establish exactly what marketing research is and how it can be used.

WHAT IS MARKETING RESEARCH?

Marketing research involves two important research activities:

product research: finding out whether the service or product you provide is appropriate; or **market research**: identifying your 'markets' or client groups and deciding what will motivate them to take up your offer.

Typical questions or problems that marketing research will help solve are:

- ❓ should we launch a new service, and if so, what?
- ❓ should we target a new client group?
- ❓ why has there been a change in the numbers or types of people using a particular service?
- ❓ what will be the effect of altering a current service?

WHY DO MARKETING RESEARCH?

You may feel that answers to some of your questions can be adequately guessed at, or that having a discussion with colleagues will produce enough information to make a decision. But there is no substitute for ensuring that you have sound information. Few organisations can afford the mistakes of wrongly targeted promotions, of services provided in the wrong place or wrong way, or of discovering that the audience they thought was there just isn't interested.

Marketing research can:

- reduce uncertainty in decision-making and therefore risk of failure;
- help plan the details of an effective marketing strategy;
- analyse and monitor the success of the chosen strategy.

The South Bank Centre undertook both qualitative and quantitative research in order to find out who did and did not use its facilities, and why. A quantitative analysis of ticket sales revealed it was appealing mainly to the A, B, C1 social groups. Qualitative, attitude research revealed that this was mainly due to ignorance of the centre's location and activities by other groups. Armed with the research information, the South Bank Centre was able to target a wider audience and develop a marketing strategy to reach them and persuade them to use the facilities.

Effective marketing research consists of four stages: establishing your **objective**, deciding your research **plan**, putting it into **action**, and carrying out a **review** of the results.

- Your research **objectives** are the result of deciding and clarifying what the problems or questions are that you want answered.
- Your research **plan** is the most cost-effective way to find the answers to your questions.
- Your action is carrying out the research.

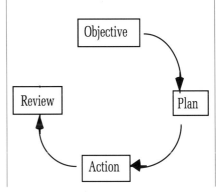

- Your review should see if you have answered the original questions. If not, you may decide on further research.

Let's look at each stage in turn:

SETTING OBJECTIVES

Two examples should illustrate what this involves:

A health authority needs to do some long-term planning of care for the elderly in its area. Its research objectives will be to: establish population forecasts for the next five and ten years; find out what other agencies providing services for the elderly in the area are planning; find out what services carers of elderly people, and elderly people themselves, would like to see developed.

A community group is campaigning to stop a proposal for a new housing development. Its objectives will be to find out which other local groups they can gather support from, and what impact the planning proposal will have on different interest groups in the area.

What information is required?

Never do marketing research simply because something would be 'nice to know'. When done properly, research is far too costly in time or money for this. This means that before undertaking any research exercise you must be sure of *what* information is required and *why*? Ask yourself:

? What decisions and action will the information lead to?

? Is this information really needed or is it an excuse to delay making the decision?

To check what information is really necessary to move your organisation forward outline your marketing research exercise using this page as a guide. First, identify a decision you need to take that will affect your long-term activities. Then fill in the sheet under the following heads:

Objectives: (What do you need to know to take a particular strategic decision?)

Method: (How will you obtain the information you need – e.g. questionnaire, group discussion, observation, check internal records?)

Resources and costs: (How much time and money will your research take? Can this be justified given the information you are likely to find out?)

PLANNING

Planning your research means deciding the most effective and least costly way to find out the answers to your questions.

You can find information from a variety of sources; the trick is to find the most cost-effective. So if the answers to your questions have already been published in a report or are available from your own organisation's records then that is your first stop. This is called **secondary** or **desk research**.

Sometimes the information is not available either from your own records or other published sources. Then **primary** or **field research** will be needed. This may involve designing a questionnaire, observing what goes on, or interviewing an 'expert' in the field.

Depending on your research questions you will be seeking **quantitative** or **qualitative** information. Quantitative information is that data which is quantifiable: sizes of client groups, amounts of time or money spent, number of visits, etc.

Qualitative information is everything else! It includes identifying why people behave in certain ways and hold particular beliefs and attitudes.

Secondary research

Every day your organisation collects information about your clients, about developments in your area of work, or the activities of other organisations. Information is collected also by a huge range of other organisations; and reports and articles published in great numbers. Central and local government, education and health authorities, tourist boards, trade associations, and private research bodies spend many millions each year on research, so there is a strong possibility that someone, somewhere already has the answers to some of your questions.

The best sources of free secondary information are:

Your own internal records : What records do you keep of past clients, users, members, or donors? Can you improve any of your record-keeping systems to give you more information on them in the future? For example, a museum wanting to know more about its visitors could introduce a visitors' book. Other useful internal records include:

- phone call logging forms
- till receipts
- logging attendances at meetings
- client or member record cards.

These records show the numbers of clients and users and the types of people they are.

If data from internal records is not sufficient and doesn't answer all your questions then you'll need to turn to information from outside sources.

Public reference libraries: Particularly reader-friendly reports, giving a broad overview of and trends in a wide range of different sectors are Mintel, Keynotes and Euromonitor.

Government departments: National government conducts an enormous amount of research. Ask for details at your main local library or business library.

Local authorities: spend huge amounts of time and money on researching economic and demographic trends. The planning, economic development, and social services departments are particularly useful.

Universities and colleges: Geography, sociology, economic, arts, and business studies departments all conduct research and might even conduct a survey for you.

Trade and professional associations and trade unions: conduct various research projects on behalf of their members. Sometimes their reports are reserved for members only, but they may provide a summary if requested.

Other institutions: such as the Arts Council, CBI, local Chambers of Commerce, and the English Tourist Board regularly report on trends affecting their sectors.

*Market research agencies:*If your budget allows you may be able to purchase general reports on market trends from market research agencies. The Market Research Society will help you identify them.

The many sources of secondary information will provide you with an overview and statistics about your market at a very cheap cost. However, it is important to check the information to find out how reliable and how current it is.

Primary research

If secondary sources of information do not provide sufficiently specific answers to your questions then primary or field research is the next step. Here's an example:

> **The Sikh community want to decide how to attract second and third generation Sikh youth. Influenced by the West this younger generation find the traditional religious ways**
> **unattractive. The Sikh community might ask the youth to complete a questionnaire whilst visiting the temple. Questions will include:**

- What is unattractive in the way the temple is currently run?
- What other facilities do they want?
- When would they use the facilities?
- Would they be prepared to pay for them?

Depending on how representative the answers are, the Sikh community can make decisions on what new facilities to provide, how much it would cost and the membership which would result from the changes.

Alternatively, a museum might want to know at what level to price souvenirs in its shop. In this case a visit to various competitors and an observation of their prices will give an indication.

Primary research is specifically geared to the information needs of your organisation but because of this it is costly to collect.

Some of the more common ways of conducting primary research are:

- observation studies
- self-completion or postal questionnaires
- telephone interviews
- personal interviews
- group discussions
- test marketing.

Your choice will depend on the objectives of your research and on your budget and time constraints. If you need quantitative data, for example how many people and what types of people use or will use your facilities, questionnaires are the most popular way to ask. If you need qualitative data, for example why people behave in certain ways and hold certain beliefs, it is important to meet up with respondents face to face, either individually or, for more in-depth discussion, in a group.

Observation studies

Useful when the information required is observable and when the observer has an opportunity to write information down. For example, recording how many and what type of people frequent a café in a museum.

In some public buildings, such as libraries, electronic devices are used to monitor numbers of visitors.

Advantages: You save time not having to communicate with the group you are observing.

Disadvantages: You can only observe what is happening, not find out why.

Self-completion or postal questionnaires

These can be completed by visitors to your location or sent in the post to clients or members of your organisation. You may decide to include a questionnaire in a members' newsletter, or accompanying an invoice or letter.

Advantages: This is a cheap way to collect information as you do not need to employ an army of interviewers.

Disadvantages: The response rate can be very low unless there is a good incentive for people to return the questionnaire. For example, an arts centre might say: 'All completed question-naires will be put in a draw to win 10 lots of free theatre or cinema tickets.' Also, you need to keep an up-to-date mailing list of the people you want to send the questionnaire to. Enclose a stamped addressed envelope, or some other incentive, to encourage response.

Telephone interviews

Advantages: Cheapness, by using the phone, you cut down on travelling time. You can cover a wide geographical area, make lots of notes without putting off the respondent. You can explain a question if it is confusing and enter the answers directly onto a computer analysis package.

Disadvantages: You may be interrupted if the person being interviewed is called away from the phone. Some people do not welcome being phoned. Check first! Some people may be permanently unobtainable or fob you off. Also not all people are on the telephone.

Personal interviews

People can be interviewed on the street, in their homes or offices. Use questionnaires to conduct street interviews – they should not last longer than three minutes. For interviews at people's homes or offices, you can ask specific questions that you have written down or chat around a subject with a guideline of the particular topics you want to cover.

Advantage: With interviews in people's homes or offices there is an opportunity to develop a rapport with the respondent/s so they feel able to talk more freely.

Disadvantage: Unless you are careful, the way the you ask the questions may dictate the answer, for example by your tone of voice or the emphasis you put on a particular word.

Group discussions

You can find out why people, perhaps current or potential clients, behave in certain ways or their opinions on certain issues by setting up and facilitating a group discussion to explore their views.

Test marketing

You may be uncertain about making a prototype product or service more widely available. If so, it is possible, and sometimes most appropriate, to launch the activity or service in a limited way, perhaps at one location or for a limited period, and carry out research at the same time to test users' reactions.

Sampling: how many people do you need to ask?

If it is too expensive and time-consuming to contact every person in the group/s you want to question, you can select individuals from that group. However, the sample should be as representative of the whole group as possible to ensure that your results are accurate.

Random sampling

If you can identify each member of the group you want to question from the phone book or the electoral register, then you can use the **random** method of sampling. Here's an example:

A museum wants to sample the views of all of its Friends. The total number of Friends is 1000 and the museum decides it would like to get the views of 50. Dividing 1000 by 50, the museum must contact every 20th person, first randomly choosing a number between one and twenty, say four, and then by contacting the 4th, 24th, 44th, etc. person on their database by phone. Had it decided to send a self-completion questionnaire through the post it would have needed to send more than the sample number, as not everyone would have responded.

Researchers often need to carry out sampling at random within a number of clearly defined groups, a technique called **stratified random sampling.** For example, suppose a health authority wants, to contact health education units, GPs and members of the public. In this case it will need to select a random sample, using a method such as noted above, from each of these groups.

The characteristic of a random sample is that each person in the group has a chance of being selected. This is not so for quota sampling where the interviewer choses the respondents to fit predefined quotas.

Quota sampling

If you are not able to identify all the members of your group by name, you can obtain a more representative sample by breaking down the total group to be questioned by meaningful characteristics such as age, sex, or occupation. This technique is called **quota sampling**.
For example:

A religious organisation wants to find out why young people do not attend prayer meetings. It decides to break down the total number of young people in its community by age:

	14–19 year	20–25 years	Total
boys	25%	30%	55%
girls	20%	25%	45%
Total	45%	55%	100%

They then decided to ask a sample of 1000 young people. Taking into account the proportions of the whole young community, 20% or 200 of the young questionned must be 14–19 year old girls, 25% or 250 must be 14–19 year old boys, and so on.

The interviewer is then free to pick interviewees until the quota for each group has been achieved.

Designing a questionnaire

Once you have decided on your sample you may need to design a questionnaire to obtain the data you want.

Before even thinking about the specifics of the questionnaire, check back to your objectives. If your objectives are clear you should be able to answer:

[?] Who you are asking
[?] What you are asking i.e. what you need to know
[?] Why you are asking i.e. how will knowing this information help us?

If you are clear about the answers to these questions you can begin drawing up the questionnaire itself.

Wording your questions

When drafting a question always ask yourself:

[?] Will the respondent find it easy to answer?
[?] Will it be easy to analyse the response?

It will help if the questions:

- follow through logically from one subject to another
- cover only one point each
- use only language that people are familiar with
- allow space for the answers
- are as simple as possible
- avoid being leading or taxing people's memory too much.

There are four types of questions, three of which simply require ticks or crosses in the appropriate box as answers:

Questions with yes/no/don't know answers:
Does your organisation hire video films for staff training programmes?

yes [ ]   no [ ]   don't know [ ]

Questions with multi-choice answers: The principle here is that if there are a limited number of likely replies then identify them for the respondent to save them thinking! For example:

Please tick the appropriate box/es.

How did you hear about our theatre?

Newspaper advertisement [ ]
Newspaper review [ ]
Local what's on guide [ ]
Our programme leaflet [ ]
Word of mouth [ ]
Other (please state) ....

Scaling questions: These ask the respondent to agree or disagree with a series of propositions or to rate them in order of importance or relevance:

If the theatre introduced a matinee performance on Mondays, how likely would you be to attend?

Very likely [ ]
Quite likely [ ]
Not very likely [ ]
Very unlikely [ ]

How important do you rate the following when choosing what hospital to use:

Competence of staff

Very important   [ ]
Important   [ ]
Somewhat important   [ ]
Unimportant   [ ]
Very unimportant   [ ]

Comfort of bed

Very important   [ ]
Important   [ ]
Somewhat important   [ ]
Unimportant   [ ]
Very unimportant   [ ]

Open-ended questions: These require respondents to write down in full their opinions, satisfactions and dissatisfactions with your project, service, etc. Though comparatively easy to compose, these questions demand a lot from your respondents, who may have little time or inclination for completing a questionnaire. Use them sparingly!

Apart from the questions, **don't forget to include:**

Survey identification data: Give the survey a title and put on the name of your organisation to make the questionnaire look more formal and stop it getting lost.

Introduction: Introduce your organisation and the reason for doing the questionnaire. Thank the respondent in advance for taking the trouble to answer and assure them that their opinions are valuable to you. If appropriate, offer an incentive to complete and return the questionnaire.

Respondent information: At the end of the questionnaire, in order to make sense of the answers you have gathered, you will need to classify the person responding in a useful way. This may be as detailed as a name and address, or their sex, age, occupation, the post code where they live or work.

Instructions: It is essential to give clear instructions for completing and returning the questionnaire. Don't forget to include:

- the return address (at the end)
- details of which questions to be omitted under which circumstances
- details of how to respond to a question: by a tick, cross or writing a full answer.

ACTION

When you have planned your research you'll need to resolve certain practical considerations before it can take place.

CHECK:

[?] Who will ask the questions or send out the questionnaires?

[?] Where is the best place to reach respondents – at your own location, at the respondent's home or office, on the street or elsewhere?

[?] How much is the research likely to cost in time and money?

REVIEWING YOUR RESULTS

Remember that the only reason for undertaking research is to gather information that will allow your organisation to make progress.

Look back to your research objectives. The information you collect should go some way to filling in the gaps in your knowledge, allowing you to answer your questions and proceed.

Manual analysis

Where you have asked multi-choice, yes/no and scaling questions you can analyse them by simple counting. Answers to open-ended questions are more difficult to analyse but comments can be made meaningful by listing them under broad relevant headings. Here's an example:

An arts centre might ask:

Are there any services you would like us to provide that we do not currently offer?

Broad headings:

- a bookshop
- a café
- a record shop

The answers to some questions are more meaningful when analysed jointly with the answers to another, often a respondent information question. For example:

Your age
21 under	[ ]
22–30	[x]
31–40	[ ]
41–50	[ ]
51 +	[ ]

On this visit did you go to:

the poetry reading	[ ]
the classical music concert	[ ]
the theatre	[x]

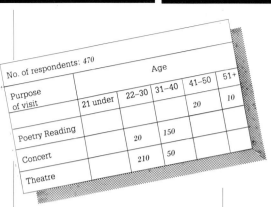

No. of respondents: 470	Age				
Purpose of visit	21 under	22–30	31–40	41–50	51+
Poetry Reading		20	150		
Concert		210	50		
Theatre				20	10

No. of respondents:	Age				
Purpose of visit	21 under	22–30	31–40	41–50	51+
Poetry Reading					
Concert					
Theatre					

When all the questionnaires have been analysed you may find something like:

From this you can deduce which age groups are attracted to which facilities and which age groups are not being attracted at all.

Computer analysis

There are several computer packages designed to analyse questionnaire information. To allow this analysis, computer codes have to be attached to each possible response on the questionnaire. A computer consultant can advise on the relative merits of the different packages available.

Results

Don't forget how important it is to write up your results clearly. You can present them in table form, followed by a brief report. As in the questionnaire, clarity, simplicity and brevity are the key!

Finally, it is not enough to acknowledge the results. At the end of a marketing research exercise you should be thinking about action. 'We can now make the following decisions.' 'We will now make these adaptions or improvements to our service.'

TEMBA'S AUDIENCE

Our research shows that the typical visitor to our play is 18-35 years old, reads The Guardian, The Times, The Independent, Time Out, City Limits, The Voice, The Caribbean Times. The typical adult Temba theatre goer is in full-time employment or further education, is reasonably affluent, is a car-owner and dines out around once a week. About 30% of our total audience is made up of school children, youth workers and teachers. Our present marketing strategy aims to increase both the audience base as well as paid attendances.

SUMMARY

Marketing research can reduce the uncertainty of selecting which route to follow, to help plan the details of particular services or projects and help you to monitor the success of your chosen strategies. But before embarking on research make sure you have thought through in detail:

- *your research objectives*
- *your research methods*
- *the research itself*
- *how you will review the answers.*

Finally, remember the golden rules of marketing research:

- *Ask: 'What can I learn?' not 'How do I prove I'm right?'*
- *Do a little often, rather than one-off monster surveys*
- *Check the information you need is not already available*
- *Make the questionnaire/discussion fun. Don't pry, offend or confuse.*

Once the results are analysed and you have the answers to your questions, act on what you learn!

CHAPTER 3

Contents   Page

Client groups 28
Donor groups 29
Decision influencers 30
Summary 31

Introduction

The key groups of people for your organisation to take into account when planning a marketing strategy are:

- **clients** or potential clients – the people you want to influence or appeal to
- **donors** or potential donors – the people or organisations that will provide the resources
- other members of the public who, because of their seniority or particular relationship with your donor or client groups, will influence whether clients or donors end up supporting or using you. These are called **decision influencers** and may be clients or donors, work colleagues, friends, or parents, depending on the decision to be made.

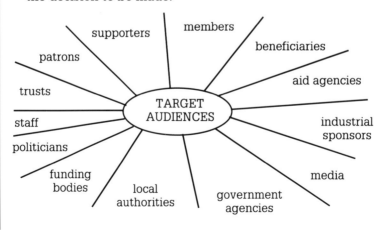

It may seem difficult, as a non-profit organisation, to tie down who your clients, donors or decision influencers really are. It is important, though, to both identify and understand them quite clearly in order to offer appropriate services which respond to their needs or to communicate in a way that will appeal to their interests, desires and concerns.

This chapter will help you identify:

- your client groups and their needs
- donor groups, whose support you will need to continue your work in terms of volunteer time or a cash donation
- the influencers who will affect their decisions.

CLIENT GROUPS

If you take your target audiences into account at an early stage of planning your marketing campaign, activity or service then you can be more certain of providing effective and useful services. This in turn will justify your existence to funders, supporters and other influencers.

How do I identify client groups?

You may want to offer your service or send your message to every citizen in your town or city. Unfortunately this takes resources, time and money that non-profit organisations rarely have access to. So it is important to identify which citizens you are best placed to reach, given your skills and limited resources.

- Do these people have needs or interests in common?
- Are they a certain age?
- Do they live in a particular location?
- Are they employed or unemployed?
- Are they a mixture of these?

This process of banding together clients who have similar requirements but who differ from the general population is called **market segmentation**. It enables your organisation to:

- develop products, services, adverts or information that more accurately respond to these clients' requirements, therefore satisfying clients and making the most effective use of resources
- focus its marketing activity on those clients whose requirements are most compatible with the organisation's resources.

For example:

The Nelson and Colne Drop in Skills Centre (DISC) was designed to meet the requirements of all adults aged 16–65 years who wanted or needed to learn new skills on an 'off-the-peg' basis. DISC provides technicians, work stations, tools, equipment and courses to suit a variety of different professions: plumbing, electrical work, computer and typing skills.

Market segmentation involves two stages:

- describing the characteristics of each segment
- finding a method to capture their support and attention.

In marketing terms you need only approach one group of clients differently from another if they need to receive different information or services from you.

For example:

The Sikh community, when deciding what activities to organise in their community centre will look at the different interests which may vary according to age and gender. Activities will be devised according to the needs and interests of those target groups that the community particularly wants to attract.

Here are just some of the ways in which you can segment and describe your target clients:

- location
- age
- occupation
- income
- family size
- social class
- lifestyle, or attitudes or interests, etc.
- stage in the family life cycle
- age
- sex
- marital status
- education
- religion
- ethnic origin.

[?] How might you break down your clients into useful groups?

What do your client groups need?

The purpose of segmenting your target audience into smaller groups is to be able to reach them and communicate with them more effectively. Communicating the right message depends on finding out what will motivate them to use you.

[?] List the different **client groups** you have identified. Note what **needs** each of these groups have in relation to what you offer. Then think how well you can **satisfy** them given your current resources.

The trade union GMB found that its appeal and membership were flagging. It segmented its client groups by gender, age, and occupation and analysed the needs of each. The results of the analysis showed that it was not meeting the needs of all its new members. These were new, emerging groups which the union's original formation had not accounted for.

Therefore GMB modified its message in a way that would begin to appeal to the new women and minority group workers whilst not alienating its traditional male dominated membership.

As decribed above, needs may vary from one group to another. However, these needs can also change with time. Are you confident that your organisation is aware of and meeting the specific needs of your target group, and that changes in these needs have not passed you by?

Back copies of women's magazines show how women's attitudes have shifted over time. Although the contents of the 1950s and 1980s editions are vastly different, a large proportion of the readership consists of the same individuals at both periods. The message from both these cases is: keep checking to make sure your target group hasn't moved on and left you behind!

DONOR GROUPS

Just as there is a range of clients who you will want to take up what you offer, there will be a number of organisations who will provide the resources (goods, services, facilities, money, time, energy) that will allow you to carry out your stated objectives.

Donors might include:

- members of the general public providing money or time
- trusts donating money
- industry donating goods, money, expertise

- statutory organisations providing grants, accommodation, etc.

? Who are *your* donors? Make a list now of both your *current* and your *potential* donors.

Your donors' needs

Donors usually provide resources in return for what they see as value for money. This value might be in the form of:

- good PR – being seen to be associated with your organisation
- testimonials from satisfied clients
- updates on numbers and types of people assisted
- reports on your efforts to keep costs under control.

Donors often need their name to be put 'in lights'. For example, American Express (AMEX), in joint promotional efforts with St John Ambulances, needed to make sure that the public knew it was AMEX who were supporting them.

? What information or results do you present donors with?
? Is it enough?
? If not, what more might you provide?

DECISION INFLUENCERS

When identifying your client and donor target audiences it is also crucial to be aware of who makes the decision to use your services or fund your cause, and how this decision is made.

For every decision made by your target clients or donors, there will be a series of people they refer to for information, advice and the authority to go ahead. They may include:

- **the information collector** – the person who looks at the options available
- **the financier** – the person who writes the cheque
- **the final decider** – the person who has the overall power to make a decision
- **the pusher** – the person who wants to make the decision

but does not have the authority to do so
- **the consumer** – the person who will gain benefit from what is offered.

In the world of commerce, marketing strategists identify these people as being the influencers or as making up the **decision-making unit**.

The Main Influencers

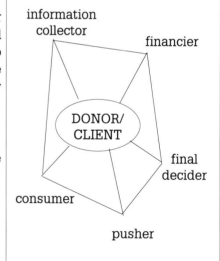

Think of how you might make a decision to join a trade union. Although you will be the person who becomes a member there will be other people along the way who have assisted you in making the final decision. When joining a trade union, your final choice may be dictated by:

- your employer, who may demand you join a particular union or prevent you from joining a union at all
- your colleagues who may recommend or criticise the unions they belong to.

These are the influencers and the trade unions will need to take them into account when communicating with their target audiences.

> The Trowbridge GP maternity unit wants to promote itself as the unit for normal births. It considers how the decision to use it or the high-tech unit in the town centre is made.
>
> The decision-making unit here may be as follows: The pregnant mother wants the best in care. So does the husband. The family doctor – the pusher – recommends the GP unit. The consultant at the unit, the ward sister along with other mothers who have had successful births there – the influencers – endorse the decision. The pregnant mother – the decider – decides to use the GP unit. If there is no opposition, the pregnant woman may be the 'final decider'. Finally, there is the financier, in this case the National Health Service, who pays for the birth.

Clearly it is important that each member of the decision-making unit is informed about your service, and is aware of all its benefits. The approach has to appeal to each member's interests. Think through how decisions are made to use your service or contribute to your funds. Then list the various people and organisations who can influence your target market to decide to come to you.

SUMMARY

No one organisation can provide services to meet the needs of the whole population, nor could any single organisation afford to. In order to operate successfully, each organisation will look to fulfil a particular role by providing services or directing a message at groups who express the same needs, attitudes or interests.

When planning your marketing strategy you should now make a habit of:

- *defining very clearly and specifically who your target markets are*
- *segmenting your target groups*
- *checking out in detail the different interests and needs of your clients and funders*
- *identifying and appealing to the various individuals and groups who take part in the decision-making unit.*

Armed with this information, your organisation will be well placed to design services and offers that appeal to your clients and funders, and to put your message across efficiently and effectively.

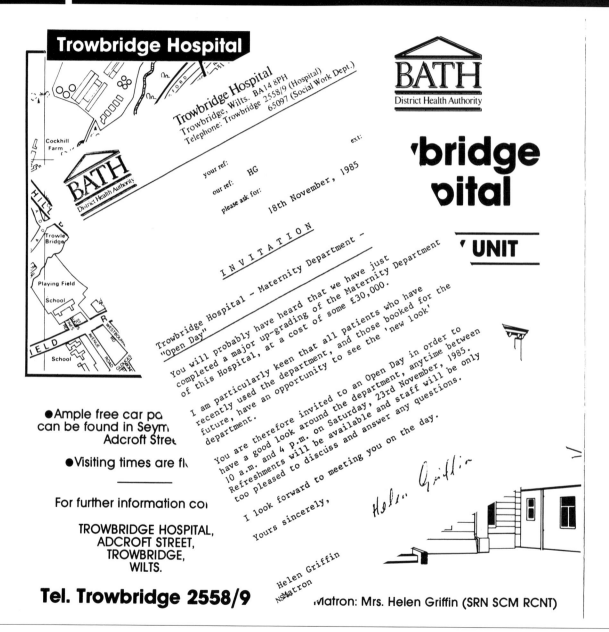

Trowbridge Hospital

Cockhill Farm

Trowle Bridge

Playing Field

School

School

Trowbridge Hospital
Trowbridge, Wilts. BA14 8PH
Telephone: Trowbridge 2558/9 (Hospital)
65097 (Social Work Dept.)

BATH
District Health Authority

your ref:

our ref: HG

please ask for:

ext:

18th November, 1985

I N V I T A T I O N

Trowbridge Hospital – Maternity Department – "Open Day"

You will probably have heard that we have just completed a major up-grading of the Maternity Department of this Hospital, at a cost of some £30,000.

I am particularly keen that all patients who have recently used the department, and those booked for the future, have an opportunity to see the 'new look' department.

You are therefore invited to an Open Day in order to have a good look around the department, anytime between 10 a.m. and 4 p.m. on Saturday, 23rd November, 1985. Refreshments will be available and staff will be only too pleased to discuss and answer any questions.

I look forward to meeting you on the day.

Yours sincerely,

Helen Griffin

Helen Griffin
Matron

● Ample free car pa
can be found in Seym
Adcroft Stree

● Visiting times are fl

For further information co

TROWBRIDGE HOSPITAL,
ADCROFT STREET,
TROWBRIDGE,
WILTS.

Tel. Trowbridge 2558/9

Matron: Mrs. Helen Griffin (SRN SCM RCNT)

CHAPTER 4

Contents   Page

Your product   35
Your price   39
Your place   41
Your promotion   42
Summary: your total offer   42

Introduction

Your total offer consists of what you provide your target audiences. What this is will depend on:

- the variables that we mentioned in Chapter 1, such as political, economic, or social changes. These are largely outside your control.
- variables within the control of your organisation.

There are four main **controllable variables**:

- the resources used in the creation of your services, facilities or activities. We'll call this your **product**.
- the **price** – if any – you charge for receiving what you offer.
- the accessibility of your location, or how effectively you organise the distribution of what you offer. We'll call this your **place**.
- how effectively you inform clients, potential clients, donors and other important people about what you offer, in other words, your **promotion**.

These four variables, your product, price, place and promotion can usefully be remembered as 'the four Ps' of the marketing mix. Together with the marketing research you do, they are the marketing tools your organisation has at its disposal to design effective strategies to reach and affect your target audiences.

This chapter will examine each of the first three elements in turn. It will help you organise your:

- product
- price
- place

in order to achieve your objectives as effectively as possible. The final 'P', promotion, is a major topic in its own right and we are therefore giving it a chapter to itself (Chapter 5).

YOUR PRODUCT

You may feel you don't have a product as such to sell. But a 'product', whether intangible like a religious way of life or tangible such as a publication, is **whatever you have to offer your target audiences**.

To design an effective product marketing strategy, you need to know:

- what your product is
- the key factors that determine the nature of your product.

What is your product?

To clarify what we mean by 'product', let's take two examples, from Nelson and Colne College:

- **The Drop In Skills Centre**
  The *product* this centre offers its clients is the opportunity to learn new skills by providing easy access training facilities, manuals and tutors.

  The *clients* are unemployed people living in the area or those in employment who want to up-grade skills or retrain.

- **The Technology Express bus**
  The *product* is a service which introduces the public to new technology ideas and equipment on a bus packed with computers and software packages. The *clients* are staff at schools, local council housing estates and businesses.

▣ Now decide what product you offer. Is it:

- a physical product
- a service
- a space or facility
- an event or experience
- a social situation
- an idea or philosophy
- a way of life
- expertise or skills
- written information or advice
- something else?

You may of course find that you are offering more than one of the above.

You may also be offering a product not only to clients, but also to donors. The product to them may be an information up-date, a monitoring of the take-up of services, and feedback on the effectiveness of services provided.

What factors determine the nature of your product?

The nature of your product will be very much shaped by:

- the resources available to your organisation, your skills and facilities – refer back to the strengths and weakness analysis in Chapter 1
- the needs of your target audiences
- what the competition is offering
- uncontrollable variables: the political, legislative, economic and cultural factors that may affect what you can offer.

Let's look in more detail at each in turn.

Your resources

A hospital may want to give a personal caring service to every one of its patients but if there are staff shortages this is unlikely to happen. What it must do is market effectively the service it *can* provide.

Always base what you offer on the resources, the funds, the income, staffing levels, skills and facilities that you can reasonably expect will be made available to you. Your targets should always be achievable.

The needs and requirements of your target audiences

If you design what you offer with the audience/s it is aimed at in mind, it is then much easier to market it.

If you examine your product in more detail you should be able to identify which features particularly appeal (and which are problematic) to particular client groups. Remember that 'features' covers a wide range of possibilities:

> The features of a theatre performance include:

- content of programme
- location
- performance times
- admission price
- seats, room, environment
- theatre's reputation, name
- performing company's reputation, name.

> The features of a charity's fund-raising campaign include:

- organised activities
- a letter requesting money
- a leaflet/brochure identifying why the money is needed
- charity's reputation, name
- an amount to be donated.

For some organisations adapting the product to suit a target audience may be easy; but others may feel that if they adapt their product they will lose the whole aim and purpose for which they exist. Such an organisation doesn't scrap its product because it lacks popular appeal, but perseveres because the ideas it hopes to introduce are for the greater good of society. The challenge is to find ways of influencing behaviour or attitudes so that eventually they will appeal.

> The Anti-Smoking lobby has used different campaigns over the years, some more successfully than others. At first they tried, through media advertising, a direct appeal to smokers to abandon the habit, and then appealed to the smokers' vanity through the Ashtré and Stub perfume campaigns but with limited success. Finally, they appealed to the smokers' social conscience by highlighting the effects of secondary smoking on their families, and enlisted the support of the non-smoking community to create a force for change.

What the competition is offering

In order to justify its existence your organisation needs to stand out in some way from any other related ones. If there is nothing to distinguish you from the competition in the eyes of your target audiences, then you should

HAVE A HEART

PLEASE DON'T SMOKE

ON WEDNESDAY 9 MARCH 1988

National No Smoking Day

'Helping people who want to stop smoking'

[?] Now describe the distinguishing features of your own product using the following prompts as a guide (this list is not comprehensive and some of the descriptions may or may not be appropriate to your offer):

Feature	Appropriate for audience ?	If inappropriate how to modify?
your location		
your price		
the quality of staff assistance you offer		
the amount of staff assistance you offer		
the written information you provide		
your accessibility		
the availability of what you offer		
your opening times		
the subject of your performance/meeting/ publication		
the number of your staff		
the skills and abilities of your staff		
your facilities/equipment		
the content of your message		
your name		
your reputation		
the layout or design of what you offer		

consider merging activities and efforts and benefiting from the economies of scale.

Two charities working with the elderly might fulfil very different roles:

Charity A may be involved in organising holidays, workshops and friendship clubs around the country. Charity B may be involved in lobbying Parliament to change legislation relating to the elderly. Their relative positions can be depicted as follows:

organising activities to improve quality of life

Charity A
x

not involved ___ involved in
in lobbying   lobbying

Charity B
x

no involvement in organising activities

Consider how your organisation differs from others working in a similar area or with a similar group of people. Does your target audience clearly identify this difference?

Uncontrollable variables

Finally, you need to consider the effect of uncontrollable variables on what your products look like. It's easy to turn a blind eye to these – until you find that what you offer is no longer wanted. So make a point of considering:

- relevant current affairs
- legislation
- media stories
- technological developments.

Discuss the implications of these at planning meetings. Even if your organisation is very small it should be possible to find a member willing to keep a look out in one of the national dailies.

Product life-cycle

One way of considering the effect of variables is to think in terms of the product life cycle. Almost all products tend to go through this cycle, but with widely differing speeds. For example, the lifespan of a drop-in skills centre for unemployed people would be seriously reduced if the employment situation were to recover dramatically. The centre would have to adapt to survive. In some cases, the need continues to exist for a very long time. Healthcare, for example, is in the maturity stage and it will probably be a long time before demand declines. But specific methods of treatment may have a short lifecycle. Education, too, is in the maturity stage, but learning by rote has long been in decline or obsolete as a teaching method. It is important to recognise that an idea, method, campaign, or service, may be of considerable importance in one decade, yet obsolete the next.

Stages in product life cycle

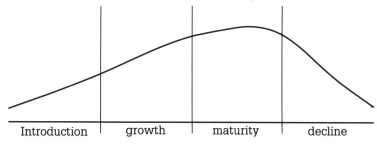

| Introduction | growth | maturity | decline |

Can you identify at what stage of the life-cycle your product is? If one aspect of your work is no longer required, do you have another area to develop or which is growing in popularity?

Summary: designing a product strategy

Products or services born of customer needs and requirements are more likely to be appropriate and satisfactory. You then need to let customers know these exist and how to obtain them.

The key points to remember when designing your product are:

- consult your target audiences to identify what type of service they need
- modify your service to meet those needs
- ensure you are clearly distinguishable from your competitors
- keep a close eye on any uncontrollable variables that may affect you.

Having looked at the first P, your product, let's move on to the question of price.

YOUR PRICE

There may or may not be a monetary price attached to what you are offering. However, in any exchange of goods, services, or ideas there is a price to be paid. This price may be paid in money, time, energy, thought, a change in behaviour, attitudes or life-style. There is a cost or price attached to anything you offer, both to your organisation and the person taking up your offer.

Offering free entertainment in a theatre foyer costs the theatre:

- **staff time**
- **the space taken up, which cannot be used for another purpose**
- **performers' fees.**

To the spectator, the cost is:

- **the time they give up**
- **the energy they spend by attending**
- **the cost of the transport and perhaps babysitting charges.**

When planning your activities, however 'non commercial', you should always ask:

- Can your organisation afford to do it?

and, when applicable:

- Can the client afford to pay the price attached?

What price do your clients pay?

If you want people to take up your product, then it is important to make every effort to ensure that the price is affordable: payable, and accessible both to your audience and to your organisation.

If you do not weigh up the costs involved, your target audience certainly will. If your offering is too expensive they may choose an alternative one or, where no alternative exists, may do nothing at all. For example, if the wait at a doctor's surgery is too long or too inconvenient then a client may choose to visit the local hospital's out-patients' department, consult their pharmacist, make a self-diagnosis, or ignore the problem.

When choosing between various options, people will look at the **opportunity cost**. This refers to what opportunities you give up by pursuing one option in preference to another. For example, if the two options are a visit to the cinema or a visit to the theatre, then the opportunity cost of visiting the theatre is your visit to the cinema, since there is insufficient time to do both.

Your audience needs to judge your price to be reasonable and affordable. You can demonstrate the fairness of the price by showing that you have taken their needs into consideration when planning your offer. Local authorities, for example, give leaflets explaining how the rating charges have been arrived at and showing clearly the value each ratepayer gets for his or her money.

If you are not getting the response you would like, it may be that you are charging too high a price.

If the price is very high

As we've already noted, the price clients have to pay may be measured in money, time, effort, or a habit they give up. Where the price to be paid is very high, then it is important to recognise this and try to soften the blow. The Health Education Authority did not simply demand that people stop smoking but created opportunities such as National No Smoking Day.

Working out an appropriate monetary price

There are three steps to setting an appropriate price:

1.   Calculate the cost of providing what you offer, including rent, rates, light, heat, staff costs, promotions budgets, etc.

Some organisations will add a pre-determined percentage to this amount and leave their prices at that. This is called **cost-plus** pricing. However, this price might bear no relation to what is going on outside of your organisation. Therefore marketing sense says take two further steps:

2.   Examine   what   your competitors are charging for a similar service. Depending on how you compare on quality, speed of delivery, and so on, you will set your price lower, higher or the same as theirs. Certainly, if you offer a far superior service, then your price ought to reflect this.

3.   Examine what the clients are prepared to pay. Attitudes to prices can be quite complex. In some cases we want 'value for

money' and won't be prepared to go above a particular limit. In other cases, we may be prepared to pay more, if we believe that what we are being offered is somehow better quality than other services. Sometimes, if a price is very low, we mistrust the offer, and think that there must be something wrong with it, or that the quality is inferior.

Bear these things in mind when setting a price.

Pricing tactics

You can choose the pricing tactic which best suits your financial objectives:

Loss leader: offering a part of your service free or very cheaply to draw people in. The South Bank Centre offers free foyer entertainment, to encourage people to come in. They may well be encouraged to attend a performance, or spend some money in the bookshop or the café.

Price lining: offering a service at a range of prices to denote the different qualities available, for example, theatre seats at different prices.

Discounts: Season tickets can be used to encourage regular attendance by offering substantial discounts. A museum pass will allow the holder to visit several exhibitions, thus fulfilling objectives concerned with increasing regular visitors.

Differential pricing: offering the same service at different prices to different target audiences according to their ability to pay.

If you have a monetary price, how is this set at present? Is this in line with what is being provided by other organisations? Is this in line with your clients' expectations?

YOUR PLACE

The third part of your strategy is the question of place: how people obtain your product – whether they come to you, or whether you have to find ways of reaching them.

Any activity, service, or facility you offer must be available and accessible to your target audiences if they are to take up your offer. Whether you contact clients by placing an advertisement in the newspaper, shaking collection tins in the street or making a product available through local shops will depend on:

- their needs
- how accessible you are to your target groups
- your resources.

Client needs

We've already described how Nelson and Colne College used a 'technology bus' to sell its services to a geographically dispersed target audience who would not have time or the inclination to enrol on college courses. The college also developed a user-friendly 'drop-in' skills learning centre which was accessible and provided a positive environment to all those in the surrounding area wanting to improve and learn practical skills.

In the first case, the disadvantage of location was surmounted by taking the service to the people; and in the second, accessibility was enhanced by approachability – meeting people's needs in an informal manner.

Some local authorities research the users of their facilities to find out how far they are prepared to travel, and how much they are prepared to pay in travel costs. This gives a measure of the value of the facilities, even where entrance is free.

Accessibility

Factors to take into account when reviewing your location are:

- geographical accessibility: is there adequate car parking, public transport?
- physical accessibility: what arrangements have you made for disabled access?
- mental/perceived accessibility: are there plenty of signs, information signs and arrows inside and outside your building? People like to know they are in the right place. If you have a reception area, make sure there is always a staff member willing to help and offer friendly assistance.

Your resources

You may want to deliver your product to your clients' doorsteps. However, this demands a high level of resources. You may find that budgets dictate instead a central location that people visit, for example a library. A middle path is a mixture of the two. For example, a general practitioner will hold surgeries *and* make house calls; a priest will call at people's homes *and* welcome the congregation to the church.

If your product or service is distributed to your clients, whether by post, out on the streets (e.g. people collecting for charity), or through the wholesale and retail network, then your considerations will be different, but will still revolve round making your offering as available and accessible as possible to your target audience. Research your intended audiences, pinpoint where they live, send your offering directly or identify outlets in the area that you can supply.

? Is what you offer accessible to your target audience:

- geographically
- physically
- mentally?

If your answer to any of these is 'no', take steps now to ensure that you make the necessary changes.

YOUR PROMOTION

Whether people come to visit you, or you take your service or facilities out to them, they have to be made aware of what you are offering and how to get it if they want it. This is achieved by careful targeting of client and donor groups and telling them about what you have to offer in language that is appropriate and understood by them. This is the fourth P, promotions, and is the subject of the following chapter.

Before moving on to Chapter 5, check that you have now:

- identified your product
- checked that your product features will motivate your audience to 'buy'
- placed your organisation in relation to your competitors, saying how your group is different
- planned an appropriate price for your product or worked out the cost to clients in taking up what you offer
- ensured that your product is as accessible as possible to your audience.

SUMMARY: your total offer

Your total offer to each group of clients is the mixture of the product features, the price, the distribution network or place and the promotions that will be most appropriate and attractive to them. Remember though that you are not totally able to control what is offered as your strategy will be partly shaped by the uncontrollable variables, your competitors, the political, social environment, and so on. Your role, therefore, is to make what you offer as responsive as possible to your audience's requirements, given the external constraints that surround you.

CHAPTER 5

Contents

Contents	Page
Drawing up a strategy	45
To whom: your target audience	45
Why: promotional objectives	45
How: promotional methods	47
With what effect: feedback	52
How much will promotion cost?	52
When should I promote?	53
What: your promotional message	53
Summary	58

Introduction

The fourth 'P' or marketing tool at your organisation's disposal is your **promotion**, or how you make target audiences aware of what you are offering. Promotion is essentially about communicating. In the broadest sense, well-typed letters on headed notepaper, tidy premises, friendly staff and a good telephone manner are all aspects of promotion because they communicate a particular message about what you stand for.

This chapter looks at how to use the main promotional techniques to communicate successfully with your clients. It will help you:

- clarify your message
- select the right medium
- choose appropriate objectives
- reach your target audience
- obtain feedback about your promotional activities.

DRAWING UP A STRATEGY

Successful promotion depends on successful communication. A clear grasp of the communications process is the first step in planning a well-thought-out promotions strategy.

We can represent the six key factors of communication as follows:

[?] Who is saying what, how, and to whom?

[?] What do you think was the promotional objective behind this communication?

[?] In your opinion, how successful is it in terms of communication?

These six features form the backbone of your promotional strategy. You'll notice that references to objectives and target

1. **WHO** (the source):   Your organisation

2. is saying **WHAT** (the message):   This may be a slogan, or a longer description of your service

3. **HOW** (the medium):   Adverts, posters, press release, etc.

4. **WHY** (the objectives):   To raise funds, sell tickets, etc.

5. to **WHOM** (your target audience):   Donors, clients, influencers

6. with **WHAT** effect (feedback):   Monitor the results of the promotional activity

Using this model, analyse any piece of promotional material which has recently come to your notice:

audiences keep cropping up. This is because effective promotion on a limited budget requires clarity about what you want to achieve, and who you want to reach with your message. Let's look at some of these in more detail.

TO WHOM: YOUR TARGET AUDIENCE

A clear knowledge of your audience will determine *where* you promote and *what* you say, and the tone and language you use.

One of Manchester City Library's objectives was to encourage members of the Chinese community to use the library service. They used leaflets, posters and signs inside the library printed in Chinese to explain the library services available.

You may want to address several different target groups simultaneously, for instance, clients and influencers, to promote a particular service. St John Ambulance uses joint promotions with AMEX, including events, to reach a wide variety of target audiences including volunteers, funders and donors.

WHY: PROMOTIONAL OBJECTIVES

You need to be clear from the start about what you want your promotions to achieve.

You will then have:

- a yardstick for judging whether a particular type of promotion will help you reach your goals
- a target against which to monitor the actual effects of your promotions.

? What do you want your promotions to achieve? Decide now. Do you want them to:

- promote an event
- sell your product/service
- raise donations
- stimulate interest in your service
- educate people, change attitudes
- build the image of your organisation
- other?

The objectives for your particular campaign will depend on:

- what you want from your target audiences
- how much they already know about you
- how interested/supportive they already are towards you.

One way to tackle these variables is to use a trick of the trade called

AIDA. This is an acronym for Attention, Interest, Desire, Action. It works as follows:

ATTENTION: if your organisation is totally new, then your first objective is to attract the attention of your target audience. Your promotional strategy must be designed to get your name about and raise your profile.

INTEREST: at this second stage you want to stimulate people's interest in your work, and through the information you provide show how your work is relevant to them.

DESIRE: the third stage requires a slightly different message. Here, your aim is to create a desire in people to participate, join, or support your cause.

ACTION: the final stage should prompt your audience into taking action by returning tear-off slips, freepost cards, etc.

A poster advertising a theatre performance or a new library service are excellent ways to raise awareness. Adverts with cut-out coupons and direct mail-shots enclosing freepost envelopes for donations will encourage action.

HOW: PROMOTIONAL METHODS

There are hundreds of different ways to communicate with your target audience. However they fall into four main categories:

- advertising
- public relations
- sales promotion
- personal selling.

Your communication is likely to be most effective if you use a mix of these methods. For example, if you are a charity requiring business sponsorship you might send a letter (advertising), then follow this up with a phone call and visit (personal selling).

The particular combination of methods you choose is your **promotional mix**. Its aim should be to build up awareness from no knowledge of you or your product to a clear understanding of what your organisation does.

Choosing which promotional techniques to use will depend on:

- what you want your promotions to achieve
- what your target audience is likely to hear/see/read
- your budget.

Advertising

Advertising includes all paid-for forms of advertisement including media adverts, newspapers, magazines, billboards, radio, television, the sides of buses. Also leaflets, posters, brochures and direct mail letters.

Media advertising

Outdoor and transport advertisements are excellent for raising awareness, and image-building. Adverts in newspapers and magazines, where coupon or phone numbers are included, can be very useful for raising donations or selling a service direct.

All these forms of advertising are good for putting over short, punchy messages.

Advertising rates vary tremendously, and there may be discounts for charitable organisations, for block bookings, or for late night adverts on local radio. Ask about discounts, always negotiate, but remember, when choosing the whole purpose of advertising is to inform, and if your audience does not read that particular paper, listen to that radio station or live on that bus route, then perhaps you haven't got such a good deal after all.

Checklist for advertising in the media

Check the *British Rate and Data Publications Directory (BRAD)* in your local reference library for publications relevant to your organisation.

Check in *Yellow Pages* under 'Advertising – outdoor' and 'Advertising – poster & transport' for the outdoor and transport options available to you locally.

Select the particular newspapers and magazines you feel will be most likely to reach your target audiences. Phone their advertising department and ask for their media packs. These contain readership profiles, circulation figures and advertising rates. Any publication worth advertising in should have one or at least be able to tell you who and how many read it.

If you produce a brochure or journal, you might consider producing a media pack for prospective advertisers, telling them about the size and characteristics of your audience.

Make sure that the reader or viewer profile as specified in the media pack matches that of your target audience.

If your various options look equally appropriate calculate the comparative costs of reaching 1,000 readers or listeners.

> **For example, at the time of writing the circulation of a local paper is 10,000, the cost of a half-page advertisement is £100, therefore the cost of reaching 1,000 readers is £10. Use this formula to check the cost per thousand per half-page in other journals to find the most cost-effective options.**

Check on the discount structure. When are discounts offered?

Are there different rates for different positions in the paper?

Be wary of hidden charges. Ask about VAT, charges for camera-ready artwork.

Posters, leaflets, brochures, inserts

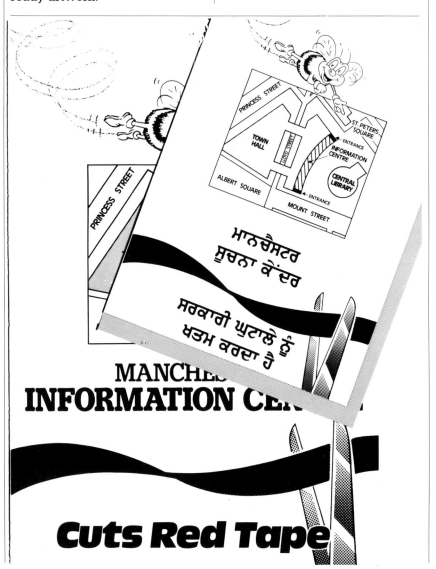

You must decide how your poster, leaflet, brochure is going to be used before commissioning the design and printing. Size is a make-or-break factor – if your poster is too large, shopkeepers and café owners might be unwilling to commit all their display space to you at the expense of other organisations. If you want your brochures to be displayed on the shelves of public libraries, etc. then check first that your proposed size will fit on those shelves. This may seem a small point, but it's crucial if your expensive material is not to lie forgotten behind the librarian's desk.

The main costs here are printing and artwork. However, distribution also costs money, whether you post the material or pay someone to distribute it for you, so do include it in your budget.

Direct mail

You can use direct mail letters to direct requests or pieces of information at specific individuals. You will need an up-to-date list of names and addresses which will come from your own records, from organisations reaching the same target audiences or from professional list-brokers.

Checklist for direct mail-shots

Whether your list of names and addresses comes from inside or outside your organisation, ask:

- Is it up-to-date and are all details complete?
- How often is it updated?
- Is there a contact name provided?
- Is the named contact person the person you want to speak to?
- If you are renting the list from outside your organisation, ask:

  – What is the cost of each thousand names and addresses and the minimum number you have to buy?

  – Do the names and addresses come on self-adhesive labels, and is there an extra charge for this?

These will give you an indication of how useful the list is.

Public relations

Unlike advertising, **public relations**, or **PR**, is a continuous activity which you can use to build a favourable image, raise awareness and create goodwill. Practising good public relations within your organisation will not necessarily cost a lot of money, but it will take time and effort to carry it out successfully.

You'll find it useful to separate PR into two broad areas:

- everyday public relations: dealing with the public on a daily level, particularly for organisations with an open-door policy.
- press and media relations: dealing with journalists.

Everyday public relations

Carrying out public relations involves communicating the image your organisation wishes to project to its target audiences. Feedback is especially important here, to check that any messages you send out are received and correctly understood.

You can set up this dialogue with your target audiences by:

- attending conferences to make contact with your public
- public speaking, which is a tried and tested method of telling people what you want them to know about your work
- publishing a newsletter and inviting contributions
- organising a properly structured channel for complaints, i.e. a person or department or address to whom suggestions or complaints can be directed
- if possible, reserving one telephone line or extension for information and enquiries.

Trying to build up your image through events and activities is fine, but your efforts will be in vain if people get an unhelpful reception when coming face to face with your organisation.

? How do your receptionists answer the phone?
? Are they welcoming?
? Are your staff courteous, helpful to visitors?

The following points will help ensure that your target audience gets the right reception.

Answering the telephone:

- be positive, helpful, efficient and cheerful. Don't keep callers holding on while an obscure bit of information is located.
- take their number and tell them you'll call them back. Do call them back!
- when you are making the call, use a script or a list of questions if the call is likely to be complicated.

Reception

First impressions count, so make sure the public gets the right impression by keeping your premises tidy, and your staff friendly and efficient.

Press relations

If you have a newsworthy story, or think that your organisation or activities will fit well in a particular feature section of a newspaper or magazine or a TV or radio programme, then pursue this by contacting the relevant journalist or editor.

When dealing with journalists:

Do

- organise your thoughts so that you can give them a coherent and concise story
- lay out your press release correctly – it saves them time and makes them more likely to use it – example in next section
- follow up your press release with a phone call to check it has arrived and to persuade them to use it
- find out when their deadlines are
- be certain of the information you can make public and what should remain confidential.

Don't

- lose your cool if you are being interviewed aggressively. Stick to your previously prepared facts
- talk to unknown journalists on the phone without finding out their reason for calling.

Sales promotions

The term **sales promotions** covers one-off promotions such as money-off vouchers, competitions, free gifts and other incentives. These are heavily used in the commercial world when the objective is to encourage the 'desire' and 'action' stages of the decision-making process. You may find that some of these are useful to you, whether or not you make a charge for your product.

Cut-price offers – half-price/two for one/buy one, get one free – can entice people to try you for the first time. Competitions can be used to increase take-up, collect information by asking entrants to say 'what they like best about your project is …', or even to inform the public about your organisation by including information about you along with the competition details. Free gifts and promotional novelties such as carrier bags, pens and ties printed with your logo can help build up goodwill by supplying something useful, while providing you with free publicity. For example, in the World Wildlife Fund's joint promotion with Anchor Butter, the purchaser can buy a special offer World Wildlife Fund gift.

Personal selling

Personal selling involves a representative of your organisation presenting your case to your target audiences either at a meeting or over the phone. This is a particularly useful approach when trying to raise money or lobby influential people, as a personal approach is likely to command more attention and interest. When communicating directly with someone you have an opportunity to answer questions and to deal with their objections. For example, Manchester libraries employed a representative to visit local small businesses to explain the marketing and research information readily available at the library.

The following table summarises the different forms of promotion we've discussed:

PROMOTION TECHNIQUES

Public relations	Sales promotions	Advertising	Personal selling
caring service	competitions	press ads ▪ local	at conferences
news releases	money off offers	▪ national ▪ special interest	face-to-face
news conferences	free gifts		over the phone
media relations		TV/radio appeals	public meetings
publicity		name on vehicles	
education campaigns in schools		brochures leaflets	
seminars		inserts	
open days		logos	
exhibition of work ▪ at your offices ▪ in public places		posters	
		outdoor/transport	
demonstrations of product use		direct mail	

Identify a particluar situation/event you want to promote.

- Which target audiences are you trying to reach?
- What do you want this promotion to achieve?
- What techniques might you use to reach them?

WITH WHAT EFFECT: FEEDBACK

If you monitor and record the effects of your promotional efforts you will begin to build up a picture of the most effective promotional techniques for your organisation.

Monitor your promotions by:

- coding your address on any promotional material you produce, e.g. 'Department xyz, World Wildlife Fund'. When people return your coupon or write to you you will know how they heard about you
- coding media advertisements. Request this of the particular publication
- including the question 'How did you hear about us?' on your telephone message pad.

Ask it of all new callers, especially when you are promoting

- (if you are large enough) organising a market research survey to monitor changed attitudes or levels of awareness
- at any events you attend where your target audience is, asking if they have seen, received, heard about your promotions.

N.B. Write up very briefly what you find out so that you can refer to it next time you plan your promotions.

How do you measure the success of your promotional efforts?

There are many different ways to measure the success of your promotions. You will need to decide which one best meets the needs of your organisation. You could:

- check back to your promotional objectives
- check the amount and quality of press or media coverage received
- check against the results of a previous campaign or year
- check you covered the costs of the promotions (if you intend to)

- check the cost of promotions per member/volunteer recruited. Is it justifiable? How does it rate with alternative recruitment techniques used? For example, the South Bank Centre proved the success of its promotions by showing that the audience had moved from a mainly A/B class background to encompassing the entire class range.

HOW MUCH WILL PROMOTION COST?

The most effective way to decide how much to spend on promotions is not on the basis of what you can afford but on what it will cost to fulfil your promotional objectives.

Use the following formula to cost your promotion:

- decide who to promote to
- decide what channels to use
- cost out these channels

Ask yourself:

- Can I afford this? If not, consider how you can achieve the same ends in a slightly less ambitious manner, e.g. a leaflet instead of a brochure.

- Can I justify the cost in relation to the likely returns: the amount of sales, the number of volunteers recruited or members made?

WHEN SHOULD I PROMOTE?

You may want to promote:

- only at certain times of the year, e.g. in relation to particular events
- steadily through the year, to build up awareness and an image for your organisation over a period of time.

Your promotional budgets may well restrict your organisation to short bursts of promotions through the year. If this is the case, use the following checklist to pick the most appropriate times. Check whether:

- you've got something to say
- you're ready to say it
- you have an event/product to promote
- your competition is promoting
- your audience is listening
- there's an important annual event in your area to link up with
- there's something topical happening to link up with, e.g.

Ethiopian appeals
- you have donors who need a thanking/updating
- you need to ensure your slice of the cake before the busy season
- you can boost sales in your quiet season

WHAT: YOUR PROMOTIONAL MESSAGE

Preparing to write

Before sitting down to write your message you need a clear idea of:

- what you want your communications to achieve – check back to promotional objectives
- which target audiences your communication is intended for
  - which group among your target audiences you are intending to focus this particular promotion on
  - what kind of message is likely to appeal to them
- what benefits these people are likely to be seeking (see below about benefits)
- which features of your organisation can offer significant benefits to these particular people

- what you want people to do as a result of receiving your communication, e.g.
  - contact you for further information
  - send in a donation
  - attend your event.

The content of your message

Selling the benefits

When clients take up products or services, what they are really looking for is the benefits these products give. The material object purchased, the service supplied is only a means to an end, not the end in itself.

> **For example, the Drop-In Skills Centre we have looked at has as its product training facilities manuals and tutors which are available through the day and evening. The clients don't attend because of these facilities but because of the benefits they can gain, that is, increased skills and confidence.**

Therefore your organisation's 'product' must be seen by clients to:

- solve a problem or
- satisfy a need.

Since people buy products for what they will do for them – that is, the benefits of using the products – then it is these benefits you should be talking about in your promotional material rather than the product itself.

[?] Refer back to your description of your 'product'. List on the table below the main features you wish to promote and identify the related benefit to the client. A simple formula to turn a feature into a benefit is to use the phrase 'which means that'.

For example, **The Drop-In Skills Centre is open till 10 p.m.** *(feature)* <u>which means that</u> **clients who are employed still have access to the facilities to retrain and improve skills** *(benefit).*

The layout of your message

To gain the attention of the people you are aiming it at, the layout for your advertisement, leaflet, brochure or poster must contain three vital ingredients, **the three Is.**

The following format will help you achieve this:

Headline – usually in bolder, larger type

Copy – i.e. main text

Illustration – a line drawing or photograph

Contact information and credibility boosters

Your organisation's name/logo

Let's look at these in more detail:

Headline

This should highlight a concern, desire, problem or worry likely to be relevant to the target audience, or identify the main benefit of them buying the product.

Aim: to create an impact, attract attention

Copy

Your copy should contain the minimum number of words needed to communicate a message that will be understood with the minimum amount of effort.

Aim: to generate interest

Product ....

Feature	'which means that'	Benefit

THIS TAPE IS NOT ONLY FREE, IT'S PRICELESS.

How much is real happiness worth? Where can you find it?

There comes a time in life when you start asking these important questions.

There are answers. "Our Heavenly Father's Plan" is a cassette tape that explains, in words and song, how our Heavenly Father has provided a plan for us to find peace and happiness in this life and beyond, through the life and teachings of the Lord Jesus Christ.

If you're at a time when finding the answers to questions about life is important, ring our free phone number. The tape is free, and the message is priceless.

0800-444-161

Manchester Mission
Paul House
Stockport Road, Timperley
Altrincham, Cheshire WA15 7UP

THE CHURCH OF
JESUS CHRIST
OF LATTER-DAY
SAINTS

Here are some additional hints on writing style:

- Use a relaxed tone and avoid being hectoring or patronising.
- Use words with as concrete a meaning as possible.
- Involve the reader in the text (e.g. by asking questions).
- Keep sentences short.
- Keep paragraphs short.
- Ensure sections of text connect coherently.
- Clearly state benefits, not features.
- Avoid repetition.
- Describe clearly what you want your audience to do as a result of your communication, e.g. you want them to:
  - *visit,* then include a map
  - *phone,* then make your phone number prominent
  - *order something* or *send money,* then provide a booking form, coupon or credit-card hotline number.

Illustrations

A picture can often support or tell your message more effectively than lots of words depending on the medium, e.g. in posters and press advertisements.

Aim: to create an impact, attract attention; to break the monotony of a mass of words

Contact information and credibility boosters

Give details of where to write to or phone. This may be either your local contact addresses or offices around the country. Credibility boosters include notes about membership of a professional association, having a good reputation of so many years' standing and so on.

Your organisation's logo

The name and/or logo of your organisation should appear on all promotional material to create a distinctive image for the organisation.

Aim: to provide information on who is offering the product

Tag line (optional)

Include concise statement of what your organisation stands for, if it is is not clear from your name. For example, VSO sends men and women to share their skills with the people of the Third World.

Designing a press release

A press release differs from other promotional material. It is not about selling benefits but *putting down the key facts of your story.* Here are some hints about presentation and content.

Presentation

- Use your headed notepaper for the first page and type in 'Press Release' at the top.
- Date your story and give it a headline.
- Indicate for whose attention it is intended.
- If you don't want publicity before a certain date/time say so by typing 'Embargoed till (date/time)' at the top. This should only be used if absolutely necesssary.
- Use one side of the paper only and double line spacing.

- Leave wide margins to the left and right.
- Add 'more' at the foot of the page to indicate that more follows.
- Use a single word from your headline, plus the page number, at the top right of any following sheets.
- Type 'ends' beneath the last line of your main text.
- Provide contact names and phone numbers for further information.
- If you wish, add a brief summary of additional (background) information beneath the main text in a 'Note to the Editor'.
- If you are arranging a photocall at which press photographers can take pictures to accompany your story, give precise details of time and venue beneath the main text.
- Get someone who didn't write/type the release to check it for accuracy.

Content

- Keep content short and to the point.
- Your headline should be relevant but don't expect it to be used.

- Try to get all the essential information in the opening paragraph – **who, what, when, where** and **why.**
- Provide at least one 'quotable quote', stating clearly who the person quoted is.
- Incorporate only those leaflets, photographs (black and white 5" x 7" or 10" x 8"), annual reports, etc. that are strictly relevant and strengthen your claims.

Imperial Cancer Research Fund
P.O. Box 123, Lincoln's Inn Fields, London WC2A 3PX

PRESS RELEASE

EMBARGOED — not for publication until:-   15 March 1988
FOR IMMEDIATE RELEASE

TRIATHALON BROTHERS TO AID CANCER RESEARCH

Watching their mother's courage and determination in fighting cancer has prompted two brothers to embark on a seven day, 430 mile triathalon between Paris and Birmingham. They are undertaking the marathon event to raise money for the Imperial Cancer Research Fund.

Their journey will take them by cycle from Paris to London, by canoe along the Thames from London to Oxford and on foot from Oxford to Birmingham. Setting off from the Eiffel Tower on April 17 they will arrive at Birmingham Central Library on April 23.

But first they are holding a 13 hour trial run on <u>Sunday, March 27</u>, when they will canoe from London to Watford via the Grand Union Canal, cycle from Watford to Coventry and run from Coventry to Birmingham.

The brothers — 27 year old Brighton Polytechnic sports science student Harry Hubball and 32 year old Birmingham outdoor education teacher Tom Lilley — are not actually brothers at all. They are cousins. But Harry's mother died from breast cancer when he was five and he was brought up by her sister Josey Lilley, who became his adopted mum.

/more

2.

Sadly, Mrs Lilley also developed breast cancer and has undergone surgery and drug treatment.

The whole family are involved in the event. Harry, Tom, Josey and brother Brian planned it while father Brian Lilley and uncle Brian Barlow will be part of the support crew on the journey. Both brothers are experienced athletes with a string of marathon and triathalon events to their credit, including the London marathon.

ICRF's Midlands region appeals organiser Maureen Tatlow said: "I think they are terrific, giving up so much time and putting so much effort into helping cancer research. We appeal to the public to support their efforts. Anyone who would like to know more about it or to donate money can talk to me at the regional centre at 27 Bridgford Road, West Bridgford."

ends

Note to News Desks: For further information contact Margaret Willson Tel: 01 242 0200 Ext 5616 (work) 0536 770851 (home) or Maureen Tatlow Tel: 0602 455205 (work) or 0522 791759 (home). Attached are routes for the pilot run (March 27) and the triathalon (April 17-23) with approximate timings.

SUMMARY

This chapter has focused on promotion. This is the fourth of the four Ps that together make up the mix of ingredients that will ensure that your marketing efforts reach the right people, using the right methods, at an acceptable price, and in an accessible place.

As a reminder, check that you have followed these key steps for drawing up your promotions strategy:

- *identified your different target audiences*
- *identified your promotional objectives*
- *chosen an appropriate channel to reach them*
- *decided on your message – it must have impact, interest and information relevant to the person reading it*
- *decided on your timing*
- *decided how you monitor the effectiveness of each promotion*
- *costed each promotion*
- *drawn up a detailed schedule for what is to be done, by who and when.*

You are then ready to draw up a marketing plan that will take your organisation forward to reach its objectives – the subject of the next, final chapter.

CHAPTER 6

Contents   **Page**

What is 'planned marketing'?   61
Setting objectives and targets   61
Finalising your marketing strategy   62
Taking action   63
Reviewing your performance   64
Summary   64

Introduction

In this handbook we have looked at the principles of good marketing. We have looked in turn at:

- reviewing strengths and weaknesses
- considering who to target
- deciding how to improve products and draw up promotional strategies.

However, before you put all this into practice it is important to bring all of these elements together into a practical and implementable plan of action.

This chapter is designed to help you:

- adopt a planned approach for all your marketing activities
- set realistic objectives for your marketing
- plan your marketing mix in relation to your target groups
- ensure you have enough time and money for what you plan to do
- review your marketing to see if it has been effective.

WHAT IS 'PLANNED MARKETING'?

Planning any activity takes time, energy, effort and thought. However, from your past experience you will know that any activity you plan in advance is more likely to succeed. This is especially so with your marketing effort: effective marketing strategies do not happen spontaneously. Success depends upon following the right procedure.

Planned marketing involves:

Planning: drawing up a logical plan in order to carry out all the marketing components discussed so far in the book.

Action: carrying out marketing activities, from answering the phone in a helpful, friendly manner to implementing a major advertising campaign.

Review: checking, after a period of time, that you are indeed achieving what you set out to do.

A planned marketing process

Your marketing process should be planned from start to finish. Its component parts should be:

Identifying your current position
- who your target audiences are
- what your product is

Analysing your current position
- strengths
- weaknesses
- opportunities
- threats

Setting objectives and targets
- objectives: what you want to achieve
- targets: what you want to achieve in a given timescale and in measurable terms so your success can be monitored

Finalising your marketing strategy
- organising your product, price, place, promotions

Implementing your marketing strategy
- carrying out the day-to-day activities involved in carrying out your marketing strategies

Reviewing your performance
- checking your performance: how well you have succeeded in achieving your targets and
- monitoring your progress along the way.

We have already looked in some detail at the first two. Here we'll concentrate on the 'action stages', starting with setting objectives and targets.

SETTING OBJECTIVES AND TARGETS

To set your marketing objectives you need to be clear about what you want your organisation to achieve. You may want to aim high, but bear in mind your limitations.

Your marketing objectives need then to be translated into specific targets, to be achieved within a certain timescale, usually one year. Depending on the nature and objectives of your organisation, your targets may be to:

- raise £x in funds
- rehouse x homeless families
- win x tribunals for clients
- sell x theatre tickets per

season

- get x mentions in the local press per campaign.

It will help you monitor how well you are keeping to target if you break down yearly goals into monthly or quarterly ones. All members of staff on the marketing team should be kept informed of how well or badly the organisation is doing.

[?] Decide now what marketing targets you should set for your organisation that will help you towards achieving your objectives. Should these be expressed in terms of monthly, or quarterly, goals?

FINALISING YOUR MARKETING STRATEGY

The next part of the planning stage is to determine how you must organise your four Ps, **product**, **price**, **place** and **promotion**, to achieve your targets.

[?] We have looked at the four Ps in Chapters 4 and 5. Now answer the following questions in relation to each

segment of your target audience. Remember you have differentiated between one audience and another because they have different requirements relating to your

offer. As you complete each vertical column, it will provide you with an outline marketing strategy to use to approach the target audience you have identified in the top box.

Your strategy in the making

Strategy	Target group –	1	2	3

Target groups

Who am I aiming my product at ?

Type of product

What product are we offering them ?

Products benefits

What benefits will this group be seeking ?

Pricing

What will be the costs to the group of obtaining this product ?

Promotions

How will we promote to this group ?

Unique selling point

How are we different from any competition ?

Distribution

How will this group be able to obtain our product ?

Finances

Before you proceed, cost out what you have decided to do. Check that:

- budgets have been allocated
- your finances can stand the strain
- you have sufficient staff, with the right skills, to carry out the work.

TAKING ACTION

You can now move on to your action stage. You'll need to keep two main points in mind:

Allocation of resources/ responsibilities: Who will do what, and when?

Scheduling: When must it be done by?

Allocating resources and responsibilities

Planning your marketing, from analysing your current position to drawing up an action plan is time-consuming but in the long term time-saving. It provides you with a direction, goals and a means of achieving them.

Once you have completed your planning the main marketing activities you will be involved in during the year are organising specific promotional activities, carrying out marketing research, and holding meetings to monitor your progress.

If you just don't have the time to carry out these tasks you might consider bringing in outside help. This can range from buying the services of a marketing research agency, advertising agency or public relations consultant to approaching graduates looking for projects to work on as part of a Masters in Business Administration course. Who you approach will depend on your budgets and the urgency of the jobs to be done.

Scheduling

Scheduling marketing activities into your year should become second nature to your staff. But be wary of underestimating the amount of time required to carry out particular tasks. Do leave a margin for error or human frailty.

For each particular activity, work out how much time and human resources it requires. What skills are required to carry out the task? Will they be available when you need them?

Agenda

1. Minutes

2. Matters arising

3. Recap on previous period's activities
    - problems encountered
    - achievements
    - remedial action to be taken?

4. Goals for the next period
    - are they still achievable?
    - problems envisaged at this stage

5. Prioritising of activities
    - what is strictly necessary to achieve our targets?
    - what is no longer appropriate?

6. Allocation of tasks

7. Drawing up work schedules

REVIEWING YOUR PERFORMANCE

You should if possible hold regular reviews to monitor how well you are meeting targets. This will help your organisation to avoid under-efficiency, or under-achievement at the end of the year.

Reviewing your progress on a regular basis highlights problems and barriers to achieving your targets at an early stage and gives you the opportunity to deal with them. You may find you have to revise unrealistic targets or reconsider the objectives you have set.

Here's a possible agenda for a monitoring meeting (preceding page).

SUMMARY

In this chapter we have looked at the main stages of marketing planning. The following checklist covers the key points and should serve as a handy reference for your organisation.

PLANNING STAGES

Current position

- *Who are our audiences?*
- *What is our product?*
- *What resources do we have at our disposal?*
- *What are our strengths and weaknesses?*
- *What opportunities and threats should we be aware of?*

Objectives and targets

- *What do we want our organisation to achieve in the next two or three years?*
- *What do we want to achieve specifically in the next year?*
- *Have these been agreed by all concerned in carrying them out?*
- *How do we measure what we want to achieve?*
- *What resources do we need to carry out these activities – staff, money, other resources?*

Your marketing strategy

- *Which target groups of our audience do we want to aim our message/services at?*
- *What product/s do we want to sell to/offer each of them?*
- *What benefits will they derive from what we offer?*
- *What promotional methods will we use? (choose from public relations, personal selling, sales promotions, advertising)*
- *What prices will we charge? (N.B. not necessarily monetary prices)*
- *What methods of distribution will be used?*
- *Where will distribution outlets be located?*
- *What resources are needed to carry out these activities – staff, money, other resources?*

ACTION STAGE

- *How will responsibilities and resources be allocated?*
- *Who will work out work-schedules, and when?*

REVIEW STAGE

- *When will monitoring meetings be arranged, monthly, quarterly?*
- *Have targets been achieved?*
- *What problems or achievements have occurred?*
- *What remedial action needs to be taken, if any?*

BOOKS

Burnett K   *Advertising by Charities*
                     Directory of Social Change 1986

Diggle K   *Guide to Arts Marketing*
                     Rhinegold Publishing 1984

Drinkwater J   *Get It on Radio and Television*
                     Pluto Press 1984

Kotler P &   *Strategic Marketing for Nonprofit*
Andreason A R   *Organisations*
                     Prentice-Hall 1987

Lovelock C H &   *Marketing for Public and*
Weinberg C B   *Nonprofit Managers*
                     John Wiley 1984

McIntosh D & A   *A Basic PR Guide for Charities*
                     Directory of Social Change 1985

McIntosh D & A   *Marketing: A Handbook for Charities*
                     Directory of Social Change 1984

Murray R   *How to Brief Designers & Buy Print*
                     Hutchinson Publishing Group 1983

Ward S   *Organising Things*
                     Pluto Press 1984

Zeitlyn J   *Effective Publicity and Design*
                     Interchange Books 1987

DIRECTORIES

Blue Book of British Broadcasting
Tellex Monitors Ltd

Benns Press Directory
Ben Publications

Pims Media Directory
Pims (London) Ltd

The Creative Handbook
Information Services Ltd

Advertisers Annual
British Media Publications

PR Planner
Media Information Ltd

Brad Directory of Publications
Maclean Hunter Ltd

Direct Mail Databook
Gower Press

Directory of Grant-Making Trusts
Charities Aid Foundation

VIDEO

The Marketing Mix – Social Variety
YTV and Channel 4. A composite tape (VHS or Betamax) of the four programmes made by YTV for broadcast on Channel 4. (This book was written to accompany the series, first shown in June 1988.) Available from: G. Foster, YTV Ltd, The Television Centre, Leeds LS3 1JS. Educational discounts available.

BBC Appeals Office BBC

Appeals assistant
The BBC
Broadcasting House
London W1A 1AA
01-580 4468 ext. 7744
For information on broadcast appeals

IBA Appeals Office

Appeals secretary
The IBA
70 Brompton Road
London SW3 1EY
01-584 7011
For information on broadcast appeals

Lifeline

BBC radio slot
BBC Studios
Elstree
Herts WD6 1JF
01-953 6100 ext. 2220
A noticeboard for charity events

Local radio

All BBC and Independent local radio stations (see Yellow Pages) have 'What's on' spots. This is a good route for publicizing your events and activities.

ITV Community Service Announcements

Many ITV companies produce community service announcements which allow voluntary and statutory organisations air time on television to promote their service or ask for volunteers. These 'free' commercials of up to 30 seconds cannot be used to ask for money or to assist with fund-raising events. Contact the community service announcements administrator at your regional ITV company for more details.

The Marketing Resource Centre

11-13 Charterhouse Buildings
London EC1M 7AN
01-608 1144
Provides marketing training and consultancy for voluntary and arts groups

The Media Project

The Volunteer Centre UK
29 Lower Kings Road
Berkhamstead
Herts HP4 2AB
04427 73311
Produces a directory of which media produce social action programmes

The London Media Project

237 Pentonville Road
London N1 9NJ
01-278 6601
Provides London-based community and campaigning groups with information and training in the use of broadcasting

Advertising Standards Association

Brook House
Torrington Place
London WS1 7HN
01-580 5555
Monitors, and advises on, standards in advertising

Arts Management Unit (Liverpool)

Institute of Public Administration and Management
Liverpool University
Roxby Building
Myrtle Street
Liverpool L69 3BX
051-709 6022
Provides courses for arts workers

Arts Management Programme (Newcastle)

Faculty of Arts and Design
Newcastle Polytechnic
Squires Building
Newcastle upon Tyne NE1 8ST
091-232 6002
Provides courses for arts workers

Arts Training Programme (Leicester)

School of Performing Arts
Leicester Polytechnic
Scraptoft
Leicester LE7 9SU
0533 431011
Provides courses for arts workers

Research Training Initiatives	18-20 Dean Street Newcastle upon Tyne NE1 1PG 091-261 6581 *Provides training and consultancy for voluntary organisations*
National Council for Voluntary Organisations	26 Bedford Square London WC1B 3HU 01-636 4066 *An advisory service for voluntary organisations; co-ordinates short courses throughout the country*
British List Brokers Association Ltd	c/o Mail Marketing (Bristol) Ltd Princess Street Bedminster Bristol BS3 4EF 0272 666900 *An umbrella organisation which can put you in touch with their member mailing-list brokers*
Workers' Educational Association	Head Office Temple House 9 Upper Berkeley Street London W1H 8BY 01-402 5608 *Provides courses independently and in co-operation with universities, local education authorities and voluntary organisations. Contact your district office or local branch (in phone book).*